My Lover

"There's Another Man In My Life"

by

Dr. Marian E. Blair

ISBN: 0-9679367-9-9

Library of Congress Control Number: 2002094992

Published by:

Divine Life Publications
Post Office Box 31099
Capitol Heights, MD 20731
(301) 218-9085
www.divinelifeworship.org

Printed in the United States by:
Morris Publishing
3212 East Highway 30
Kearney, NE 68847
1-800-650-7888

Table Of Contents

Preface

When I was a little girl, about five years old, my grandfather would always call me to his lap and say, "Ain't you a luvva?" I wasn't sure what he meant by the word being so young. That word, "luvva" sounded kind of vulgar I thought. "No grand daddy" I would reply, "I ain't no luvva." "Well, he would chuckle, Don't you love your mommy and your daddy?" "Yeah I do," I would always reply. "Well then, that makes you a luvva." He seemed to get a big kick out of saying that to me and I could never answer him with a firm yes when asked the question because he made the word lover sound like a bad word.

Years have passed and so has my grand daddy. I realize now that his words were prophecy to me after all these years. I am a lover in the purest of sense. The world has tried to make the word "lover" explicit, dirty, and sinful. However, the great love God has for me and I for him has made me complete, satisfied and whole.

This book is not written as another how to book, but rather a story about how one woman's hunger for love was satisfied by a loving, caring God. It is not an expert treatise about love or even the final word on the longing in each of us. The story is no more an authority on the subject than a romance novel or a beautiful poem or song in which the author is only attempting to relate his love experience with another. This love story however is real and not fiction. It isn't made up or simulated from someone else's experience.

It is the hope of the author that some inspiration will be transferred to the reader to desire a closer more intimate relationship with God. He is the ultimate *lover*.

Dedication

This book is dedicated to the one whom my soul loves. I give all praise and glory to Him who has drawn me to Him with cords of love. I also dedicate this book to my husband, of nearly 30 years, Apostle George Blair, who has been a vessel of God's love to me. I love you very much.

I thank Deliverance Temple Ministries, all my children, and the Body of Christ to whom I dedicate this book. I love you all.

About the Author

Dr. Blair began her walk with God when she totally surrendered her life to Him on November 21, 1975. She was baptized in the Holy Spirit and called by God to preach His word in 1978. She ministered in the choir and taught Bible Studies in her local church. She also organized and held Prayer and Bible Studies on her secular job.

In 1984 her ministry was transformed when she went out on the street corners of Washington, DC and Maryland with her husband, Apostle George Blair to feed the hungry and preach the Word of God. The experience helped prepare her and her husband for the founding of Deliverance Temple Christian Center Ministries.

Since 1984, she has served as Missionary, Evangelist, Teacher, Choir Director, Lead Vocalist, Church Musician, Secretary, Co-Pastor, and joint Overseer and Founder of Deliverance Temple #1, Capitol Heights, MD; and Deliverance Temple #2 Pinetops, NC. She is Co-Founder and Executive Director of Regeneration Development Group, Inc., a non-profit organization which ministers to the needs of disadvantaged individuals. She has studied the Bible extensively and has attained a Doctorate of Sacred Theology Degree from Family Bible College, Baltimore, MD. Her ministry has taken her, along with her husband, to many cities throughout the United States, the Caribbean and parts of Europe.

Dr. Blair and her daughter Kimberly combined to form the mother and daughter singing duo Generations II. In their first project, "Generations II, Revealed" they were urged by the Holy Spirit to minister with songs born from their personal experiences with God. Each song was taken directly from the scriptures. As a result, many have received deliverance through songs on the project.

God has gifted Dr. Blair to minister deliverance to physically abused women and those bound by substance abuse. Her gift was perfected on the streets, in the church, and in her home as she personally ministered to addicted and abused women who were sent to North Carolina from Washington, DC and Maryland. Her other areas of ministry also include the gift of governments that rests upon her particularly in the area of finances and organization.

Dr. Blair and husband, Apostle

George Blair, have been married since 1972 and are the parents of five children, 11 grandchildren, and numerous spiritual and god children who affectionately refer to them as "Mom" and "Dad."

My Lover

"LISTEN! MY LOVER! LOOK! HERE HE COMES,"

Song of Solomon 2:8a

Chapter 1

The Test of True Love

"Place me as a seal over your heart, like a seal on your arm: for love is as strong as death; its jealousy unyielding as the grave. It burns like blazing fire, like a mighty flame. Many waters cannot quench love; rivers cannot wash it away. If one were to give all the wealth of his house for love it would utterly be scorned." (Song of Solomon 8:6-7 NIV)

I was in an intimate prayer on December 31, 1975. A few members had gathered together at a Nazarene pastor's home praying in the New Year while it

1

The Test of True Love

rained and snowed outside. The tranquil atmosphere was disturbed by a phone call from my husband. He had attended a wild New Year's Eve party and now his car had broken down. I tried to keep a straight face as he yelled obscenities over the other end of the phone demanding that I come to pick him up.

I excused myself from the prayer and nervously drove to the party. While driving I prayed to God to avoid a confrontation. After all my husband did not sound like a very happy camper and it was evident that he was blaming me for his misfortune.

Arriving at the party, I was met by him outside in a drunken rage. He demanded that I get out of the car and as I complied I was met with a right hook that sent me reeling into the mud. I lay there for a minute while a thousand thoughts raced through my mind.

Now any other time during our three-year marriage and five-year dating relationship, I would have counteracted with some punches of my own. It didn't matter that I weighed less than 115 pounds compared to his 200. But this time something was different. I had found God just one month earlier. I was now changed by a newly formed love relationship with Jesus. The closest comparison I had to relate this to was like having a new love interest. I was not willing to compromise this type of intimacy. Whatever I had to do to please the one I loved, I was more than willing to do it.

Why didn't God stop this confrontation? I had asked as hard as I could ask and was really praying as earnestly as I knew how but had not avoided this confrontation that I dreaded. Would I still serve a God who would let this humiliating event take place? Believe it or not, these questions never entered my mind. I wasn't religious and had not learned how to perform as the good Christian woman at church and then act like my old self at home. The test for true love was now being performed in two areas of my new life in Christ.

True love is genuine. As defined in Webster's, to be true is to be real and not false, to be in accordance with the actual state of things. This was the type of love that was being tested, real genuine love.

3

The Test of True Love

Did I have true love for God or was it just a temporary love chill that ran down my back that day? Did I believe that His love for me was genuine enough for me to totally trust Him no matter what? If I really loved him, then I would get up off the ground and do whatever He said to do instead of what I wanted to do. Equally, if I believed God had genuine love for me then I would not have any fear about the outcome because I would trust in that love to take care of me no matter what was happening now.

As I lay praying I was fully enveloped with his love for me. I was completely overcome with such a powerful love, that I find it hard to even put into words. All I can say is that the love constrained or compelled me to tell God that I was willing to endure even this for Him if required in order to love and serve Him. (Being such a young Christian I did not know that those words would have such an impact on my life in the years to follow). Having finished my prayer, I stood up expecting another blow but he only pushed me into the car and it was over. That would be our last physical confrontation.

Even though I went home in tears and

4

cried all night, I felt the arms of my lover comforting me. There was so much that I didn't understand about God and His Word. But one thing I did have a very clear understanding about was I knew that I was deeply loved by God and that I loved him too! This was my joy and my song.

When Abraham was tested on the mount, he proved that he loved and obeyed God more than he loved his only son. This was the ultimate test for the father of faith. I was tested in love and obedience. True love always endures any testing because it is as strong as death. I had rather suffer at this point than to bring any degree of separation between me and the one I loved. The test of true love and obedience rang out in God's Word to Abraham in Genesis 22:12:

"And he said, Lay not thine hand upon the lad, neither do thou anything unto him; for now I know that thou fearest God, seeing that thou hast not withheld thy son, thine only son from me."

It wasn't my son that I had not withheld from God but my will. I loved God enough to surrender my will to Him and do whatever He wanted me to do in this particular situation. I caution people not to take the same action as I did, but to listen to the voice of their Father in every situation because no two situations will be exactly alike or require the exact same actions as another. The important thing here is having a good solid relationship so that you are in tune with His voice no matter how you feel about what He tells you to do or what you may have to suffer. I will never be able to love God back the way He loves me but I **can** obey Him. I realized that even the power to obey comes from Him alone.

"If any one comes to Me and does not hate his (own) father and mother (that is, in the sense of indifference to or relative disregard for them in comparison with his attitude toward God) and (likewise) his wife and children and brothers and sisters, (yes) and even his own life also, he cannot be my disciple." (Luke 14:26 Amplified)

I thank God that I did not allow my emotions of how I felt about my husband, the situation at hand or the mud in my face and hair to affect my love, obedience and service to Him. I am eternally grateful that I learned this lesson early in our relationship so that it would not be a stumbling block to my growth and development as a Christian.

It was years later that I realized I had just passed my first initiation into discipleship with Jesus, the living Word of God. I learned to greatly appreciate the experience that placed me as a seal over the heart of God. I was near and dear to Him more than He was to me. The more I expressed love to Him, the more He would multiply His expressions of love to me many times over. I was really reaping the little love that I sowed in God.

A Prayer For Obedience

Father, I thank you for the love that you have for me. I thank you for the outpouring of your love into my heart that flows back to yours. The love you have for Jesus is the same love that Jesus has for me. Father, help me to obey your commandments so that I might continually abide in your love for me. Jesus is in me, Father you are in Jesus, and I am perfectly united as one with you.

Reference Scriptures:

John 15:9-10
John 17:23

Chapter 2

The Search For True Love

"For God so loved the world, that he gave his only begotten Son, that whosoever believeth in Him should not perish but have everlasting life." (John 3:16 KJV)

"...Yes, I have loved you with an everlasting love; therefore with loving-kindness have I drawn you and have continued My faithfulness to you." (Jeremiah 31:3b Amplified)

I was a young woman looking for love as said in the proverbial "all the wrong places" when I realized that someone was already looking for me. A woman's dream is to be found by that special someone who fulfills all her deepest desires. Some of us have an unusually large desire whose bill can only be filled by God. Now that person would be me.

I tried looking for a natural man but I was not able to find one. I had seen the terrible way my mother was treated by my father. She always wanted his love and attention but he never had time to give her any because he was always with other people. My treatment as a daughter was not much better. I grew up feeling unloved by my father and abused by my brother, and, to make things worse, I had dated and married an older divorced man. In short, I was disappointed by the examples before me while growing up as well as the example I had become. I was looking for a loving nurturing father, a loving protective brother, a husband that would love me and be faithful, a friend and lover who knew how to thrill, caress, comfort, and completely satisfy my deep longing desires. Whew! Now Almighty God can only fill an order of this magnitude. It is amazing how I felt that a mere man would be able to accomplish all this! Frustration had set in when one by one the men in my life would fall short in fulfilling my desires.

"Oh that men would praise the Lord for his goodness, and for his wonderful works to the children of men! For he satisfieth the longing soul, and fills the hungry soul with goodness." (*Psalms 107:8-9 KJV*)

I give God praise because of His love for me. Not that I love Him but that He loves me and gave His Son for me. I rejoice in His love for me and the change He has brought in my life. I praise Him because I realize that no amount of works on my part could ever equal to His love for me or be any attempt to repay Him.

The love of God empowers me to suffer willingly for His sake. His love for me keeps me humble before him and continually basking in His rays of goodness and favor toward me. I was looking for love and I found it in the right place, it was in the heart of God.

"Now unto Him that is able to do exceeding abundantly above all that we ask or think, according to the power that worketh in us, Unto Him be glory in the Church by Jesus throughout all ages, world without end. Amen." (Ephesians 3:20-21 KJV)

I have found the love of God to be extremely vast. Because His love is everlasting, there is no limit to it. One could never capture it in a box and say that this is the sum total of the love of God. Those who may try to do this, don't have a clue about God at all. He is pure love and the Everlasting Eternal One, He is my God and Nurturing Father. His Word (Jesus) is my protective brother and lover with an added bonus of his Holy Spirit who is more than I ever longed or asked for. My search for love was over.

God in His infinite ability was able to satisfy my longing soul with His goodness. The hunger for love in every area was satisfied with God through His Word. The emptiness in my heart was filled to overflowing with His goodness to me.

Over the years I have heard people describe the goodness of God by referring to a miraculous healing, some supernatural provision made such as a house or car, and deliverance from substance abuse or some other vice. My personal needs did not include any of these items. I hungered for love and nothing else.

God satisfies me with little things each day. His compassion is new every morning. Great is His faithfulness to me. Just as a husband might bring flowers home to his wife unexpected, so does my lover shower me with His little acts of love and mercy. The little things that say I love you come across in a most powerful and profound way as He shows Himself to me each day through His goodness. Believe me, He does this in a most excellent way because He is God and no one can love better. He loves me through the stranger, a friend, or even a loved one. Whenever He shows His love to me, I am constantly reminded by Him that He is the lover of my soul.

The search for TRUE love is found in the word TRUTH. Jesus made it clear about truth in the following passage:

"Sanctify them through thy truth: thy word is truth." John 17:17 KJV

One can find true love through the truth of the Word of God. It sounds a little simple but the truth is simple and yet powerful. Many stumble over the truth because they are looking for something hard or difficult that they can market and get a patent on. However, love is to be received from a God who is love and sends that message to us through Jesus the living Word of God.

Chapter 3

The Loving Nurturing Father

Good Morning Father! Those are my words to Him in the morning when I awake. I have become so accustomed to His awesome presence and love that surrounds me. Now don't get me wrong, there are plenty of times when I don't feel a thing. Being a woman, my emotions can really run wild. Some women equate emotions for true love. Even though emotions are charged when we are in love, it remains as only a small part of the total picture. Feelings are included on the list. When I lose the demanding desire for them, my Father knows that I can safely have the feelings and anything else I want without having it come between us. I can love God and obey Him whether I feel anything or not because my relationship is not built on feelings but rather trust in His Word.

My opinion may be debatable here, but I have seen so many women give themselves to ungodly men (myself included) and other things in life because the situation felt good. Likewise, I have observed how many will fail to experience the goodness of God because they don't **feel**

14

anything. My feelings always tend to get me into trouble. It is a part of wanting to see something first or in this particular case, feel something first before I believe He is what He says.

"But without faith it is impossible to please Him; for he that cometh to God must believe that He is, and that He is a rewarder of them that diligently seek Him." (Hebrews 11:6 KJV)

When I began to experience the love of the Father, my response to Him was to give myself totally to Him, serve Him and seek to please Him all the days of my life. During my entire life this was my response to love. A woman will give up her all for the one she loves. She gives up her virginity before marriage, her respect, and anything else when she believes she has found true love. I just could not confuse the mix of womanly emotions with the true love of God. If I depended on these feelings then the first roller coaster of emotions would have sent me hurtling back into the arms of the world.

Now when I learned how to not let my feelings rule or dictate to me as far as my relationship with God, He freely lets me

15

experience full emotions for Him as well as others. Now my feelings seem to be multiplied because they never interfere with my walk with my lover. I can love God and obey Him whether I feel anything or not because my relationship is not based on feelings but rather trust in His Word.

I will never forget the day when I was born into his family. My mother had died in July 1975. She was the one who had nurtured me all my life, I felt that I needed her in this stage of life more now than ever. I was newly married, had a 2-year-old daughter, I had bought a new house, and my mother was my best friend. But now she was gone at only 44 years of age and I took it pretty hard.

Three months went by and I still could not shake the depression. The rest of the family seemed to move on but I couldn't. Maybe it was because I was the youngest of the family? I had two older sisters and a brother. One day I remember approaching a co-worker "Delia" in desperation for some answers. I told her how I saw no reason for even living on this earth. I was feeling hopeless and depressed. She said, "I think you should consider doing some volunteer work that is if you're not ready to start going to church."

Well, now, I was 23 years old and had been working since 16 for MONEY! There was no way I was going to work for free. And as far as this church stuff, I was definitely not the church going type. So forget her free advice. It goes without saying that things did not improve and after another month they were actually worse.

It was now November in my new house and new neighborhood. The Pastor from the nearby church paid us a visit "Here comes that worrisome Pastor again," I thought, "He was always coming around bugging us about visiting his church." He was a white Nazarene minister and I was a young smart aleck, black, independent woman. What made him think I would want to go to his church or any church for that matter? Nevertheless, he continued to come visit. On this particular day he asked, "Would you like to come see a movie?" Well, I thought, I love movies. I decided that I would attend church that Sunday. I only wanted to see the movie. I was not ready to do or hear anything else!

17

The Billy Graham movie was very interesting. It was nothing like the movies I was used to. After the movie, I was handed a tract where the following questions were asked:

- Is your life without meaning?
- Does it feel like a void is in your life?
- Do you feel hopeless and like giving up?
- Maybe **Christ** is the answer for your life.

"My friend, Delia might be right after all," I thought. Maybe going to church is the answer. (I didn't get the **Christ** concept, I thought it meant just going to church at the time) I promptly informed the Pastor that I wanted to join the church. "Wonderful," he beamed. "You can meet me here at the church on Tuesday afternoon at 2:00." I could hardly wait for Tuesday. Little did I know that God had sent a midwife. I was ready to be **delivered.**

On Tuesday I received a call from the Pastor's wife asking me to leave my daughter with her at the parsonage before I met with the Pastor in his office. She was so

18

sweet. She and her husband reminded me of Quakers or something like that. They recently relocated from Pennsylvania to pastor the neighborhood church. She was very plain and humble in spirit just like her husband. They didn't even own a television. I thought that was amazing. After all, how could you possibly live without a TV?

I found the pastor in his office with a pile of books in front of him. He started out by asking me several questions that made me a little uneasy. I really didn't know him that well and found it hard to relate to men and white people (I grew up in the south).

He asked me personal questions. The first question was Are you a sinner? (Why I never!) He also asked me if I felt that God had been dealing with me recently? Like a lightning flash, I remembered the day I received the call that my mother had passed away. I recalled how I ran through the house screaming, "Somebody help me!" I was home alone that day but I heard a very small voice respond with, "I'll help you." I felt too guilty and unworthy to even think that the voice may have been God's. Now that the Pastor mentioned it, I saw that it was God all along. My sins came before me.

I had to admit that I was not a "Miss Goody 2 Shoes." I confessed myself as a sinner and told him that I felt God was calling me to him.

"If we freely admit that we have sinned and confess our sins, he is faithful and just (true to his own nature and promises) and will forgive our sins (dismiss our lawlessness) and continuously cleanse us from all unrighteousness- everything not in conformity to His will in purpose, thought, and action." (I John 1:9 Amplified)

What followed next was a bombarding of the Word of God. The Pastor opened the Bible and had me read many passages without any elaboration from him. After reading for a while, he would stop me and ask, "What is the Lord saying to you?" "Nothing," I retorted. He's the pastor and should know that I don't know a thing, let alone the voice of God. After reading over Revelation 3:20 he asked me where was God and I said, "In heaven somewhere, I guess." I just didn't get it. What was he trying to prove? Just tell me how to join the church and let me go home, I thought. He's the one that should be telling me what God was saying.

"He sent His Word, and healed them, and delivered them from their destructions."
(Psalms 107:20 KJV)

But thank God for His relentless pursuit to see me delivered. He insisted on letting God do his work and not interfere the least bit. He patiently continued to just let me read scriptures even though I was vividly agitated. After a while, I began to wear down. The Word was taking its toll on my spirit. Whipped and broken, I surrendered my will. Being sensitive, the pastor asked me "Where is the Lord?" "He's inside of me," I exclaimed. Tears of joy streamed down my face as the Word of God literally jumped off the pages and landed in my heart. I felt the heaviness lift off my shoulders and be replaced by a lightness that I never knew existed.

"Behold, I stand at the door and knock; if any one hears and listens to and hears My voice and opens the door, I will come in to him and will eat with him, and he (shall eat) with Me."
(Revelation 3:20 Amplified)

The pastor remained emotionless; he

passed me a tissue and urged me to pray. "But I don't know how to pray," I whined. "God will give you the words to say, he said." I will pray first and then you can follow. We prayed or let me say that he prayed and I stumbled over some words but they were so sweet and they were from my heart. I had fallen head over heels in love with **God's Word.** I thank God even today that I did not just have an emotional experience.

Leaving the office, I was walking on air. I'm in Love, I'm in Love, so much love. Love has reached my heart. Love has come into the core of my being. Oh what joy flooded my soul!

I really did look at my hands, my feet, the trees, the ground and everything else as I walked outside. Everything looked so new and different. Why it was just beautiful! "Where have I been," I thought. I don't remember things looking like this! It's amazing how good things look when you're in love.

"My lover spoke and said to me, arise my darling, my beautiful one, and come away." (*Song of Solomon 2:10 NIV*). Yes, Lord, was

my reply, I will go with you.

I wondered why no one had ever taken the time to enlighten me before about such a marvelous experience. I also wondered if maybe this was something unique that was only known by a few people. Well whatever the reason, God was living in me and I was one very happy sister! Thank you Father. I love you so much.

"I waited patiently for the Lord; and He inclined unto me, and heard my cry. He brought me up also out of an horrible pit, out of the miry clay, and set my feet upon a rock, and established my goings. And He hath put a new song in my mouth, even praise unto our God: many shall see it, and fear, and shall trust in the Lord." (Psalms 40:1-2 KJV)

My nurturing Father carefully fed me with His Word until I was birthed into His family. He nursed me at His breast with the Word of God and gave me the start I needed to stand. He did not leave me, but continued to constantly feed me with His Word day by day. His strength came into my being as He fed me and cared for me like a mother nursing her young. I had only been familiar with a mother's love in the natural. The love of the Father saturated my entire spirit, soul and body. My Father's love now surpassed any love that I felt from my mother or husband or anyone else in this world because His love penetrates deeper than any other. His love is love.

Chapter 4

The Training

"Train up a child in the way he should go: and when he is old, he will not depart from it." (Proverbs 22:6 KJV)

"...If you continue in My word, then are ye my disciples indeed; And ye shall know the truth, and the truth shall make you free." (John 8:31b-32 KJV)

I was not familiar with the role of a father while growing up. I had never received instructions or training of any kind from my natural father. Proper training is vital for the growth and development of any child. I was a twenty-three year old wife and mother who had become a child born again into the family of God.

My only concept of fatherly training was fear. I can remember running and hiding when my father would come home. I was afraid of doing anything that might displease him because he would yell at me and that seemed worse than a whipping. I recalled how I would duck from a slap when

The Training

I would come into the house late from playing outside. I was oblivious to the fact that a father could teach me or train me or have any type of personal relationship with me. Outside of the incidents mentioned above, I had no other conversations with my earthly father. He was almost a stranger in the house when he was there.

My Heavenly Father was about to take me into some of the most powerful but simple training that would prepare me for His kingdom living. He would lovingly build under me a basic foundation that would give me stability and security lasting throughout eternity.

I left the Pastor's office equipped with a Bible Study series and an English version Bible. Actually my love affair was with the Word. I had no other crutch or distraction at **this** point to steer me off course. I had fallen in love with the Word. (The religion was learned later in life, which is another story). When I started studying Romans, I read that I was saved. Well what do you know? I did not know that being saved was what had happened to me. Now I was even more excited. I had thought all this time that being saved was not having fun, any parties, long dresses and church all the time. What a dummy! But I never felt like a dummy with my Father because I was filled with his confidence. I knew that I could do anything He asked of me because He was inside of me.

The months that followed transformed me into a witnessing fool. I wanted to tell everybody about my experience with God. I wore the experience on my face and carried it in my mouth. Many would see it and fear and trust in the Lord (Psalm 40). I was leading co-workers almost everyday to the Lord. I repented before men and God. My associates wanted to know what happened to me. I wasn't even trying to be some Jehovah's witness copy trying to win someone to a particular faith. I was only loving my Jesus, yet people kept coming to me saying that whatever I had they wanted it too. My Nurturing Father would fulfill every request, as I would pray with them.

My Father would give me special assignments. I would open a large metropolitan area telephone book and be directed to a name to call. I remember being so nervous but totally unaware that I even

The Training

had a choice to disobey my Father. My heart would pound wildly when the person would answer the phone. But that was nothing compared to it almost beating out of my chest when they would actually agree to let me pray for them, a complete stranger. The calls usually ended with them in tears and asking God to live in their hearts. Their experiences were similar to my own, many of the precious souls were having some tough times and welcomed the prayer. God trained me so well. Here I was a new Christian and leading people to God over the phone. I also did door to door witnessing with amazing results. Oh how I loved to work with my Father!

I remember standing in line in a crowded grocery store one day. As I stood in line the Lord directed me to a lady in front of me. "Give her that tract that you have in your purse," God said. I couldn't believe that he wanted me to do this in front of a bunch of irritated folks annoyed by the long lines in the store. My Father continued to gently urge me on. With my heart pounding and sweaty palms I finally mustered up the courage to touch the lady on her shoulder. "Ma'am, the Lord told me to give you this," I said with a shaky voice.

Now the devil had already said that the lady was going to either curse at me or throw the tract back into my face. But she turned to me with tears in her eyes and said, "Thank you, I really needed this." I felt so stupid and humbled like I always feel when God uses me in a powerful way. She then turned around reading the tract like she had just received some type of gold gem.

The Lord again spoke saying, "I am pleased with you my child." This time his words were different. They seemed to take on a physical form something similar to warm oil. I stood in that grocery store as the words like warm oil ran down my head, my shoulders, back, and saturated every part of my being. It was the most wonderful touch that I had ever felt. The way He touched me that day has literally lasted a lifetime. Just thinking about it now revives the experience. What a powerful Father. One touch from Him and I was hopelessly hooked. From that time forth I would always seek opportunities to hear Him talk to me like that over and over again!

My evenings were filled with fellowship with my Father after work. I worked the night shift and could hardly wait to get home and fall on my knees in the quietness of the house. I would feel His embrace and His strength flowing through my being which exhilarated me after a long day of work. He taught me to pray. Oh how I love to pray to my Father. I eagerly looked forward to this fellowship every chance I got. The training I received in prayer is rooted and grounded in the fibers of my being. It is more a part of me than the potty training I received from my natural mother or the things taught to me in school.

I can remember praying real hard in my mind with such intensity. I knew that God heard me and I was praying alone so I saw no need to pray out loud. One night as I was praying alone I heard the Lord interrupt me in the middle of my thoughts. "Pray out loud," I thought I heard Him say, I wasn't sure what He had said at first so I asked Him to repeat it. The next time He said it really slow and quite clear, Pray out loud!

"Oh" I said, "I hear you Lord." From that moment on, my prayer life took off. I learned to obey Him and when I knew better, I did better.

The Training

I received expert training by the Master, in the school of obedience. I saw early on the rewards for obedience. Forget about the dog that seeks to please his master, for a dog biscuit or for a pat on the head; I had greater rewards from my Father that drew me closer and closer to Him in many ways. I was taught how to obey Him in witnessing, in living a holy and Christ centered life, in suffering, and too much more to list here because a lot of training is still taking place even after 27 years.

One of the most valuable areas of training I have received of my Father has been from the book of 1st Corinthians Chapter 13. I was desperately seeking faith during the '80's in order to keep up with the faith movement so I thought. I read about faith constantly, I owned every book there was about faith along with books about people that were known for their great faith. I also owned many tapes, some of which I would go to sleep listening to in my bed. However, even though I owned a few tapes, it was nothing compared to the small library of books on faith that I had acquired. I even developed my own library system at work. My co-workers would come to me daily and check out the faith books to supplement the

The Training

teachings that would take place each day instead of eating lunch. Yeah, I really thought I had it going on.

Then one morning without warning it happened. I was awakened by the authoritative voice of God. It was so loud in my spirit I seemed to hear it with my natural ears. I had only heard His voice one other time when He had asked me to pray out loud. Now I heard, "You don't need faith, all you need is 1st Corinthians, Chapter 13." I opened my eyes sleepily and began to repeat what He had said. It took a couple of minutes but as I became fully awakened, I said to myself, "Why that's the chapter about love." My Father had given me such a sound rebuke. I didn't need to seek faith but he wanted me to seek to love. I could hardly wait to tell the others of His revelation to me. This was good training for all of us. Everyone needs to learn to love.

I believe that all Christians should have good training from our heavenly Father. Doesn't every good earthly father train his children? This job should not be left up to the mother alone. Some areas of training should be basic for all children of God. Specific areas of training for

The Training

individuals are given according to their individual assignments. I thank God every day for basic training and general refreshing courses that have guided my life for the past 27 years. I am able to keep my body disciplined as a well-trained soldier fit to do battle in the warfare of life. I believe that without this training, I would have been one of those up today, down tomorrow, with Christ this year, and I don't know if I know Him the next year type of Christian. The training increased my boldness and strength, developing me into the child of God that I was meant to be.

"Your word have I laid up in my heart, that I might not sin against You. Blessed are You, O Lord; teach me Your statutes. With my lips have I declared and recounted all the ordinances of your mouth. I have rejoiced in the way of your testimonies, as much as in all riches. I will meditate in your precepts, and have respect to Your ways (the paths of life marked out by Your law) I will delight myself in Your statutes; I will not forget your word. Deal bountifully with your servant, that I may live; and I will observe Your word (hearing, receiving, loving, and obeying it)."
(Psalm 119:11-17 Amplified)

Chapter 5

The Protective Brother

(...and there is a friend that sticketh closer than a brother. Proverbs 18:24b KJV)

When I think of a brother, I think of someone who is always there for you. This is especially true when it's not the little baby brother, but the older big brother that you can look up to. The big brother is watching over his little sister to ensure her safety as well as her best interest. No real loving brother would let any other male abuse or misuse his sister. I may sound a little old fashioned, but having a big brother gives a little girl security because daddy could not be with her at school, at play and other places where bullies would lurk. A special bond like no other should exist between a brother and sister.

There is a story in II Samuel 13 about the bond between a brother and sister.

"And it came to pass after this, that Absalom the son of David had a fair sister, whose name was Tamar; and Amnon the son of David loved her." (II Samuel 13:1 KJV)

The Protective Brother

This is the story of how one brother (Amnon) raped his sister and how the other brother (Absalom) avenged her honor by killing him. I am not agreeing to the method that was used by Absalom, but I am struck by the strong disgust he had for another male who would defile his sister. By protecting the honor of his sister, he caused years of grief for himself as well as for David the king and the entire nation of Israel. I never read where Absalom was sorry about the way he punished Amnon for raping his sister. It is apparent that Absalom felt justified because he felt responsible for the safety of his sister.

Sometimes women are saved from hurtful relationships by the watchful eye of a brother. This type of protection also adds to the security of a young woman and can possibly save her from a lot of pain and misery. She needs all the protection she can get. She is much more vulnerable than the man is. I was just wishing that more of the men in my life could realize this fact and stop expecting me to be so strong and take care of myself. I personally did not want to take care of myself as far as protection or provision. I was tired of the men that I knew sitting back and waiting for the woman to bring home the bacon, fry it in the pan, feed it to the babies, and then not let them forget that they were "The Man."

Whatever happened to the strong man who took care of his woman. So many women these days long for that. They feel like there is so much demand on them to perform. They miss having a real man. The men, it's sad to say may feel like there is so much pressure on them and they want the woman to almost take the place of another man in helping them. The problem is usually because he is looking to the woman for his strength and help instead of looking to God so she can look to him.

Things were going pretty good for me. Ah, Witnessing, Bible Study, Prayer Meetings, Church services, not a care, right? Wrong. I was ready for another bump in the road.

My unsaved husband sat me down at the kitchen table one day demanding a showdown between my love for God and my love for him. Can you imagine him doing that? He really didn't know any better. He was brought up in the Catholic Church (somewhat) but didn't know a thing about new life in Christ. "Well," he said, "who will it be? me or this Jesus stuff?" When your marriage breaks up, just know that it will be your fault. You should have seen his mouth drop open when I announced that my choice was JESUS! Later he said that he looked upon my face and seemed to hear a voice say, "And you had better leave her alone too!"

That was the voice of my big brother. He was there to protect me from all harm. In the midst of danger all I had to do was take a stand for my God. I wouldn't deny Him so he wouldn't deny me. I had lost my fear of man. I didn't care anymore. I would have been very happy to have him walk out that door. I felt secure and protected for the first time in my life. If anyone tried any thing with me they would have to answer to my BIG brother!

Oh! How I loved the Lord so much. The love for my Lord by this stage was stronger than Juliet's love for her Romeo; nothing and nobody could tear me away from my love because it was stronger than death. Of course my husband was not finished with me yet. If he couldn't get me to denounce my Lord then, maybe, he could stop me from worshiping him. He announced that as the head of the house, I was not allowed to attend church anymore. I was surprised to hear the words come out of my mouth. "Well, do you mind if I just read my Bible and pray, I asked?" "I don't care what you read," he snarled. "You old Bible slinging Bertha!" (That's what he would call me).

I cried out to God out of the depths of my soul. And the Lord heard me (Psalm 118: 5). He answered me very early. In a few days my husband recanted his demand and told me I could attend church again. Oh the sweet smell of victory and I didn't even get my hands dirty. I had a big brother who had my back. There was nothing to worry or fret about. I didn't need a shouting match with my husband to taste the sweetness of victory. There was absolutely no need to try to have my way about it because I knew that God was going to have his way in the matter and whatever He did would make me happy.

"And whosoever shall offend one of these little ones that believe in Me, it is better for him that a millstone were hanged about his neck, and he were cast into the sea." (Mark

9:42 KJV)

It is very unpleasant to be reprimanded by God. It's better to tie a millstone around your neck and throw yourself into the sea than to offend one of His little ones. God continued to intervene in many areas of my life; and when I needed special help, I was so love protected.

After this test with my husband, I would be tested again and again over the years in choosing my love for God over my friend, and my only child. My husband is now my best friend and brother. He would later give his life to God and serve Him with all his heart. The details of his conversion are recorded in a later chapter.

I am so glad that I didn't know or understand a lot in those days. Trying to get God down to a science or formula can lead to a major catastrophe. I don't try to over simplify God, however, I never feel the need to explain Him, what He does or how He does anything. He is God and He looks after me. There is no formula outside of His word. It's just as simple as that to me.

Many times I am asked to give

understanding as a teacher may be expected to do. I have found this to be a little difficult for myself because I recognized that it is God who gives revelation and understanding concerning Himself. When I am teaching, I have found that the unseen God illuminates the hearts of His people with words that I never said or with any notes that I read from. When I am told by a student that they heard the voice of God speaking something in their hearts that I was not saying then I know that I have completed my assignment as God would have me do it. I never seek to add a lot of my own polish to what God is doing. It may seem that I am leaving a lot of information out of my testimonies but I know that the God that I am serving will fill in the missing pieces for a custom fit for all who may read this.

How far does God as our protector go? In what other ways does He protect me? Someone recently asked me exactly what were the principalities and powers that the Apostle Paul spoke of in the Sixth Chapter of Ephesians. This warfare that was waged against us sounded really serious.

The Protective Brother

"Finally my brethren, be strong in the Lord and in the power of His might. Put on the whole armour of God, that you may be able to stand against the wiles of the devil. For we wrestle not against flesh and blood, but against principalities, against powers, against the rulers of the darkness of this world, against spiritual wickedness in high places." (Ephesians 6:10-12 KJV)

This person wanted some kind of details as to the identity of these beings or people. We had been just reading this chapter for the past nine months as part of our daily worship. Now just reading this portion of scripture didn't seem to be enough to get the job done for full protection. "Maybe if I knew who my enemy was I could know better how to defend myself," it was said. After all, you need to know who your enemy is. These were my questions in reply to the inquiry:

- If you had a detailed description of all these principalities and powers, etc. would you know how to fight better? (After all, he told you to just put on the armor and pray).

- Do you really think that you can

41

come up with the perfect battle plan to defeat them?

- If God really revealed to you all the sordid details of demons and devils, do you think you could handle all that knowledge and still operate in a normal capacity without being preoccupied with that knowledge?

- If God knows who they are then He also knows what it takes to defeat them and protect you too. Why not leave that to Him and just read it the way He instructed you to?

I am confident that God knows how to give me the right instructions at the appointed time. I trust Him for protection. I do not frustrate His grace by trying to help Him out with my own ideas or thoughts. I just know that He knows what He is doing even if I don't. Sometimes what we think we want isn't what we want at all. I am glad to have someone look after me so that I don't have to look after myself. God has protected me from accidents, sicknesses, personal attacks, making bad business deals, and the list goes on. Any attempt on my part to even put up a wall around my heart to protect myself from being hurt by people will put me on the sharp rebuke list from God.

I asked the Lord one day why was He so distant from me? Whenever I prayed, I didn't feel His presence nearby as I normally did. I went for a long walk while I prayed and inquired of the Lord receiving an immediate reply from God. "I can't reach you with that wall around your heart," God spoke very plain and matter of fact. You see some very close friends had hurt me deeply and I told myself that I was going to stay to myself and not be close to anyone again. The pain was too great. "Is that the wall you are referring to Lord?" I asked. "Yes" he replied. Well, now, that wall wasn't for you Lord, it was for people. I listened as the Lord explained to me how the wall was keeping Him out too. He told me that the wall showed Him that I didn't trust Him to protect my heart. I felt that I needed to protect myself with my own little wall. Now the last thing I would want to do is block God out. No, Lord, I said, take the wall away. I don't want anything to come between you and me. I can't take it down the Lord replied, you will have to take it down brick by brick because you put it up.

The Protective Brother

The wall was removed and, needless to say, I experienced many hurts over the years. But I will never erect another wall because He is my protection. I don't need to protect myself. With any wound He is there to pour in the oil and the wine and use the experience to draw me in closer as a partaker of His divine love.

Chapter 6

The Faithful Loving Husband

My natural husband was an alcoholic and a drug dealer. He was a wild and crazy man. His favorite pastimes were driving race cars, drinking, fighting and chasing women. He had four children with three different women and one by me. At age 33 he had lived a very reckless life. He had no regard for his responsibilities. He just wouldn't pay anybody! He was nine years older than me but I was the one who made sure all the bills were paid; even the child support payments to his other children who lived with their mothers.

When I married him I must have thought that he would be like a father, big brother and husband all rolled up into one. I really didn't know what I was thinking about. I was so confused back then and very young. I met him at the very vulnerable age of 15, I married him at age 20 after experiencing three abortions and two years of living together, I just couldn't seem to get him out of my life because I was soul tied to him.

A soul tie is an emotional bond developed with another person. The soul is the seat of the emotions and the will of a human being. My reference to them at this time will be brief, but necessary to explain my extraordinary quest for love. There are many types of soul ties.

- Soul ties can be Godly (instituted by and made into a threesome tie by God).

- Ungodly soul ties (authored by man and his fleshly desires and nature).

- Other soul ties are naturally made by everyday relationships and family ties.

The natural soul tie is the one most are familiar with. We become very attached through our emotions with family, co-workers, doctors, etc. A tie can be formed with anyone that we have a close relationship with so as to open our will and emotions to them. This may seem like just human emotions but, it is also quite spiritual and can be potentially powerful. If you are a person guided by emotions and you are tied to the emotions and will of another, then they maintain a certain amount of control over you. One pull on your emotions by them is also a pull on your will because you are **knitted together**. This is one reason why a battered wife will remain with her abuser and insist that she loves him too much to leave him. Even if she **wanted** to leave him, her **will** becomes dominated by the stronger will of the other person. She has trouble understanding the reason for her seemingly self-induced suffering.

The Hebrew word (*qasher*) and the Greek word (*sumbibazo*) have both been translated as the word knit. The original words mean to bind together as knitting, and to drive or bond together respectively. The Hebrew word *qasher* is used in reference to the soul tie between Jonathan and David.

"When David had finished speaking to Saul, the soul of Jonathan was knit with the soul of David, and Jonathan loved him as his own soul." (*1ˢᵗ Samuel 18:1 Amplified*)

God used this supernatural soul tie to

ultimately save David's life from Saul. Jonathan betrayed his own father and protected David from being killed by his father, Saul. That is how powerful a soul tie can be. If it's strong enough, it will turn you against family, friends, or anyone else including God. God wants us to have proper soul ties that will draw us closer to Him. The Greek word *sumbibazo* is also translated as knit and typifies the Godly soul tie encouraged by Paul in the book of Colossians.

"For I want you to know how great is my solicitude for you--in how severe an inward struggle I am engaged for you--and for those (believers) at Laodicea, and for all who (like yourselves) have never seen my face and known me personally. (For my concern is) that their hearts may be braced (comforted, cheered, and encouraged) as they are **knit** *together in love, that they may come to have all the abounding wealth and blessings of assured conviction of understanding, and that they may become progressively more intimately acquainted with and may know more definitely and accurately and thoroughly, that mystic secret of God (which is) Christ the Anointed One." (Colossians 2:1-2 Amplified)*

The Faithful Loving Husband

We are encouraged to form Godly soul ties because of the comfort and blessings that they bring. Quite the contrary, ungodly ties bring the opposite. We can make ungodly ties with people by having intimate contact with many lovers. It is not good to have casual sex or any other type of intimate contact with just anybody. These ties not only give us misery, but they also hinder us from being fully tied with God. If not delivered, these ties will last a lifetime. Many of us are like multi-colored knit sweaters that require the surgical hand of a loving God to unravel our souls from the knitting of ungodly threads.

Now that I had a new love interest in my life, the soul tie with my husband had been somewhat broken. Though still tied to him through marriage, the bond was not as strong as the tie with my new love. My new love was first in my life and I was not shy about letting anyone know it.

I didn't have the natural emotions motivating me, I was filled instead with a Godly love for my husband to see him saved and delivered as I was. I even put every plan, scheme, and prayer I knew to work to that effect. Needless to say, all my efforts failed trying to get him saved. I fasted, left tracts on the table for him to read, and asked every Christian I knew to pray for my husband's salvation. My best efforts infuriated him. He became more and more angry because he felt that I was dismantling his manhood. After all he was THE MAN.

One day during my frustration, I suddenly received a simple but powerful revelation from God. It finally dawned upon me that I was not a savior. Imagine that. I was not the one who could save myself or anyone else. I realized that all of my efforts were futile. Yes even though I had led many to the Lord for salvation by phone, door to door, and at work, that didn't make me the savior. I was only an instrument in God's hand. I really didn't know anything about getting someone saved. I merely prayed with them and God did the work. Why was I so frustrated now? It was because my little formula that worked so well on everyone else had absolutely no effect on my own husband. I had to face the truth.

Now I had a choice to make. I could continue to make a fool of myself by trying to get him saved like I thought he should be; or go to plan B which was get upset with

God because he was moving too slow with this particular request and use my own method to religiously fix him up a little bit. Okay I confess right now that I do not like a lot of seemingly useless work. I was learning now how to admit defeat and surrender.

"Alright God," I said, "I give up. I repent before you now in trying to save my husband. **I am not a Savior.** I realize that I have been doing this on my own. I quit. He is now in your hands. You save him Lord whenever you want to and how you want to because I am resigning from this job of saving now." I meant every word that I said and the Lord knew it. I had such a peace that I really didn't seem to care if he ever was saved. I was wondering if I was growing cold or something but I later realized that God was removing the feelings and cutting the ungodly soul tie. My new godly tie of agape love allowed me to release him fully and there were no human emotions to hinder my faith.

"There remaineth therefore a rest to the people of God. For he that hath entered into His rest, he hath ceased from his own works, as God did from His. Let us labor therefore to enter into that rest, lest any man fall after the

same example of unbelief." (Hebrews 4:9-11 KJV)

Chapter 7

The Interim Husband

"O that my ways were directed and established to observe Your statutes-hearing, receiving, loving and obeying them! Then shall I not be put to shame (by failing to inherit your promises), when I have respect to all your commandments." (Psalms 110:5-6 Amplified)

Once I made the decision to let God be God in my situation, I began to see His hand immediately upon my husband. He dealt with him more profound than He ever dealt with me. It was such a wonderful and powerful move it caused fear and awe to come upon me.

It all started one night when my husband returned home from one of his drinking binges. It had to be the grace of God to allow him to make it home safe, driving in his condition. He stumbled to the bathroom and began to vomit profusely. His head went into the toilet and he was too drunk to hold his head up. He was choking. The devil said to me, "Let him choke to death, that's exactly what he deserves."

I thank God that I was totally committed to obeying my Father. I was not walking or living by the flesh or being dictated to by what my old crucified self wanted to do but, by the Spirit, which gives life. (Romans 8). Not only life to those who live by it but the life that overflows into the lives of others.

I followed the Lord's instructions to pull him from the toilet, clean him up, put him to bed and speak kindly to him. I told him that I would get him a little something to eat to settle his stomach and that he should get some rest for work the next day. He later told me that the devil said, "don't listen to her; she is only trying to kill you." But I did kill him, with God's love.

I did not know it at the time, but this would be the pivotal point in my husband's Born Again experience. As God continued to deal with him, I would not speak of it to anyone. I had said things in my earlier days of trying to be his savior and was left with egg on my face. I would say to my friends how I could see little changes in him and he was about to be saved. But each time I made a comment like that he always got worse even though at first he looked like he was coming along just fine. Well this time I had learned my lesson. I wasn't saying anything about his salvation process, if he jumped into the baptism pool and started speaking in tongues, I was not going to speak what I thought I saw happening.

Doing that kind of thing would destroy my faith. I refused to walk by sight! If I only could speak what I saw then God would turn the other way. I had to speak in faith not letting what I saw affect me one way or the other; whether what I saw was favorable or not, I could not walk by it.

The date was June 6, 1976 when my husband was born into the kingdom of God. I had only been saved seven months but it seemed like a lifetime. Since those days, we have held countless revivals in the U.S. and abroad, organized and founded two churches. My husband is an Apostle, a Prophet, a mighty man of God, and a faithful loving husband.

God has loved me through this man and given me the desire of my heart because my heart was toward him first. When my husband loves me, I feel God's love for me. He readily admits that he did not have a clue about how to love me before God came into his life. This is so true, that's why I have learned to appreciate God even more because he uses a human vessel to be a loving faithful husband to me.

Chapter 8

The One My Soul Loves

In the Song of Solomon are found some of the most powerful words of love and adoration anywhere. There are many different interpretations of the book. Some believe that it is just a book of love poems. Others believe the man and woman stand for God and his people or Christ and the Church. Another interpretation is that the woman was taken to King Solomon's court but was still in love with a shepherd back home. In the end they were united back together.

All these interpretations were revealed to me as being accurate. The woman appeared to be courteous to King Solomon. She was compliant to his wishes and flattered by his wonderful remarks of her beauty. *"Like a lily among thorns is my darling among the maidens."* *(Song of Solomon 2:2 NIV)*

There are times where she speaks fond of Solomon, but she seemed to be constantly in search of the one that her soul loved. (1:7, 3:1-4, 5:6, 6:1, 8:1)

The One My Soul Loves

Now King Solomon was a wise and wealthy man with many wives and concubines. He really had made a name for himself as witnessed by the other maidens. *"Your name is like perfume poured out. No wonder the maidens love you."* (1:3 NIV) Though he could have had any woman, he wanted her because she was special. I believe it was her inner beauty that captivated Solomon. The virtuous woman of Proverbs 31 that fears the Lord is an awesome woman indeed. Infused with the Love of God, she is greatly desirable.

It is amazing how falling in love with God can beautify a woman better than the finest clothes, the best makeup, or fanciest hairdo. The sustaining power of the shepherd was his powerful words to the woman. A woman must be sustained by words no matter what level she is on or condition she's in. God's words are spirit and life, (John 6:63). The lover sustains his beloved with words that pass knowledge and understanding.

All through the day I hear my lover whisper, "Do you love me?" I may be washing dishes or just combing my hair or just receive some small token from His hand when his voice comes to me asking, "if I love Him?" My answer is always a resounding yes, for I am always assured of His love for me. I never have to ask Him of His love for me because He tells me constantly with words too deep to utter. My whole being is satisfied as with marrow and fatness.(Psalm 63:5).

I once had a woman tell me that her husband could speak words in her ear that thrilled her down to her toes. Words are so powerful. I am thrilled to my innermost being with the words of my lover. He holds me close with the arms of His Word during trials and tests. He wipes the tears from my eyes while he constantly reassures me that I am His. As a man responds to God so he attracts a woman to him, which may account for the attraction of women to anointed men of God. This can be a fatal attraction if the woman is not first rooted and grounded in a solid love affair with God.

"Place me like a seal over your heart, like a seal over your arm" (Song of Solomon 8:6a NIV)

My deepest cries to God were answered when He placed me as a mark or signet on His heart. I am like a charm or bracelet adorning His arm. Therefore I must look good for Him which, in turn, causes Him to look good. He asked me one day not to adorn myself with pants (I do not say this in judgement about other women please). One day He simply told me not to wear them because they were coming between our relationship. You will have to understand that I actually idolized slacks and wanted to wear nothing else. He showed me some women hanging out on the street corner and said to me, "I want you to look different for me. We cannot continue in a deeper relationship until you get rid of your idol." That very day I got rid of all my pants and allowed the Lord to clothe me with His beauty. I wanted to look good for Him I wanted to please Him more than life. This was my joy.

He is my wealthy prince who has set me up as his betrothed in an exquisite penthouse, lavishing me with the finest of everything because he spares no expense at keeping me fully supplied with only the best. He wants it to be known that I belong to Him and He belongs to me. (2:16; 7:10) He is patiently waiting, not desiring love to be stirred until He pleases or until the appointed time when we are together forever. (2:7; 3:5; 8:4)

My husband was given a revelation in the form of a dream one night. He dreamed that I had a very handsome lover to whom I really belonged. In the dream he had the understanding that I was only on loan to him for a while and that my lover understood that I had to be with him as part of some type of a contract or agreement. I believe that this was the case with Solomon and the woman. She was in his courts as maybe part of some previous agreement but her real love was a shepherd. Who is my Shepherd but the Lord? I do not want for anything. (Psalm 23:1) The dream sent to my husband could have been easily dismissed, if the Lord had not given the same dream to two other people at the very same time. I was greatly moved when they all recounted of their dreams of me having a secret lover. I knew that the lover was the Lord.

"Beloved, now are we the sons of God, and it does not yet appear what we shall be; but we know that, when He shall appear, we shall be like Him, for we shall see Him as He is." (*1 John 3:2 KJV*)

The One My Soul Loves

How shall I prepare myself to meet Him? What do I need to be doing? I need to obey the first commandment and the second one that is similar to the first one.

"Teacher, which is the greatest commandment in the Law?" Jesus replied: "Love the Lord your God with all your heart, with all your soul and with all your mind. This is the first and greatest commandment. And the second is like it: Love your neighbor as yourself. All the Law and the prophets hang on these two commandments." (*Matthew 22:36-46 NIV*)

We must love God more than anything or anyone else in this world in order to achieve peace, love, happiness and joy in this life and throughout eternity. Much is being said about things that will not really matter in the final analysis. We must seek to love God and each other and stop complicating our lives with other things that will soon perish.

Fall in love with **The Lover** and prepare to be with Him forever. He already loves you deeply **and** is anxiously waiting to shower you with His everlasting love.

A Message To
The Body Of Christ

"Come away my lover...." *(Song of Solomon 8:14a NIV)*

The time will soon come when the Lover will call us all to Him. He is coming to take us away swiftly like a gazelle (8:14b). Prepare to meet Him as the only one who truly loves your soul. When we see Him, we will know Him, for we shall be like Him.

RE-ORDER FORM

To order additional copies of **("MY LOVER")**, complete the information below:

Ship to: **(PLEASE PRINT)**

Name: _____

Address: _____

City/State/Zip: _____

Day Phone: _____

___ Copies of "MY LOVER," @ $10.00 each
Postage and handling @ $2.00 _____ per book
MD State abbreviated residence) add _5% Tax

Total Amount Enclosed $_____

Make checks payable to:

Dr. Marian E. Blair

Send to:

Post Office Box 3836
Capitol Heights, MD 20791-3836